2 —
Home

Monograms

FOR THE HOME

Monograms

FOR THE HOME

KIMBERLY SCHLEGEL WHITMAN

Principal photographer JOHN CAIN SARGENT

GIBBS SMITH
TO ENRICH AND INSPIRE HUMANKIND

16 17 18 19   5 4

Text © 2015 by Kimberly Schlegel Whitman
Photographs © 2015 as noted on page 192

Published by
Gibbs Smith
P.O. Box 667
Layton, Utah 84041

1.800.835.4993 orders
www.gibbs-smith.com

Designed by Rita Sowins/Sowins Design
Printed and bound in Hong Kong

Gibbs Smith books are printed on either recycled, 100%
post-consumer waste, FSC-certified papers or on paper
produced from sustainable PEFC-certified forest/
controlled wood source. Learn more at www.pefc.org.

Library of Congress Cataloging-in-Publication Data

Whitman, Kimberly Schlegel.
Monograms for the home / Kimberly Schlegel Whitman ;
Principal photographer John Cain Sargent. — First Edition.
pages cm
ISBN 978-1-4236-4017-2
1. Monograms. 2. House furnishings. I. Title.
NK3640.W49 2015
704.9'49645—dc23
2015008007

For my grandmothers,

Myrtle Horst and the late Ruth Schlegel,

who taught me to appreciate the intricate beauty

that can come from a single

needle and some thread.

Contents

Introduction

My sheets are monogrammed, so is my silverware and pretty much everything else I own. My rule is if it's not moving—monogram it.

—REESE WITHERSPOON

Monograms have a rich history. They have given form to the art of personal expression for thousands of years.

In this day and age, when "branding" is the buzz, a monogram is a way to make a statement about your personal brand. As a way of expressing individuality many style setters, like actress Reese Witherspoon, are personalizing everything they can get their hands on from a cardigan sweater to hand towels.

In the 19th century, monograms were a sign of wealth. Fast-forward to the 1950s, and technology and the sewing machine brought monograms back in vogue, as it was easy to add a mark of personalization to everything. Whether made by machine or by hand, a monogram is an elegant way to embellish your home.

A monogram is defined as a motif of two or more letters interwoven or otherwise combined in a decorative design used as a logo or to identify a personal possession. This definition is certainly true; however, it fails to get to the heart of what makes a monogram so special. Monograms are a beautiful, tasteful, and even regal way to personalize a product. In a time when so much of what we have is mass-produced, a monogram can make something unique while adding a touch of artistry and sophistication.

In this book, we will take a look at both the history of monograms, duograms and ciphers and the way they can be incorporated into our lives today. For many, an introduction to monograms rapidly becomes a new passion. For others, it is a lifelong tradition that honors generations. Whether you're into the hip and modern or prefer more formal styles, a monogram can enhance your home and lifestyle. From entertaining to interior design, monograms play a role in both decoration and personalization.

Setting yourself apart with a monogram is a statement of your individual sensibilities and style. J.Crew style expert Glenn O'Brien recently said this on *jcrew.tumblr. com* about the current use of monograms:

> *We live in a landscape that is covered with corporate logos. If individuals are going to compete today we need logos too. The monogram is an elegant way to make your mark. It's your name boiled down to the essence, executed with graphic artistry. It's as old as the coat of arms and it was used as a hallmark in metalwork, ceramics and graphics, marking the genuine article.*

Aside from being a personal logo and advertising ownership, a monogram's touch can help us feel confident and centered. Etiquette expert, Peggy Post, who is a great-grand-daughter-in-law of Emily Post and current director of the Emily Post Institute, says they can give us a "sense of place." One of the beautiful things about technology today is that it has made the goods we need for our homes so affordable and accessible. The downside to this accessibility is that it's hard to feel that something is truly our own. When we add a personalized touch, such as a monogram, to any item, whatever the quality or craftsmanship, we instantly make it more special.

Monograms are elegant yet practical. In almost every element of our lives, from new linens and heirloom silver to stationery and candles, we can seize opportunities to personalize our possessions with a monogram. Monogram expert Summer Tompkins Walker of Walker Valentine says, "Monograms are so special because they tell a story to the past and define a person and a place." Today, we continue to celebrate the art of the monogram, its rich history and its modern applications.

> Monograms make an ordinary thing, whether it is a pillow, a napkin or a piece of paper, instantly special because of the deeply personal nature of having something emblazoned so it is uniquely yours. It creates an instant heirloom, giving something a deeper meaning that reflects time worn traditions and old-fashioned appeal in a modern and swiftly changing mass-market world.
>
> —DANIELLE ROLLINS

For men and women alike, a monogram can be a way to personalize your belongings, a way to honor a loved one, or a way to keep a motivating affirmation in mind. Remember Elvis and his "TCB" monogram? He had it painted, engraved and embroidered on everything—"Taking Care of Business!" There are wonderful examples of people using their loved ones' monograms as a reminder of special times with them. Some people prefer to use the roman numerals of a number that reminds them of an important date. The possibilities are endless, and my hope is that this book will provide inspiration for ways that you can incorporate more monograms into your life!

The Rich Tradition

A BRIEF HISTORY OF
MONOGRAMS

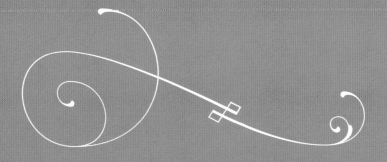

Monograms have been used for thousands of years and have certainly evolved along the way. The first known monogram was found on 6th century B.C. Roman coins. They had the initials of the ruler on them to give them legitimacy. Charlemagne most famously used his monograms as a mark of power in the 8th century. He used it to mark his conquests as he made his way around Europe. It was a symbol that showed his territories and was recognizable beyond language barriers and the various alphabets that were commonly used. Other royal and military commanders followed suit and developed their own marks, symbols of power and influence that clearly marked their ranking.

During the Middle Ages, monograms became popular among artists and artisans to mark their work. From the paintings of Albrecht Durer, who used his "AD" monogram to authenticate his work, to the marks on the underside of hand-painted porcelain, these symbolic signatures took on a new meaning. They symbolized creative pride, and more and more the monogram became the mark of a craftsman.

Also during this period, on the more practical side, markings were made to identify laundry that was done village-wide on a designated washday. Each item held the mark of its owner's family in a corner. The wealthier families in Europe possessed only the finest linens, often woven of rare fabrics and very expensive, which meant these group washday gatherings were also opportunities to show off a family's wealth. All of the linens were laid out to dry together in the countryside, so everyone could see what belonged to the other families based on the embroidered family initials. Without the monograms, it would have been easy to mix up the linens of the various households. As commercial laundry houses became more common, these

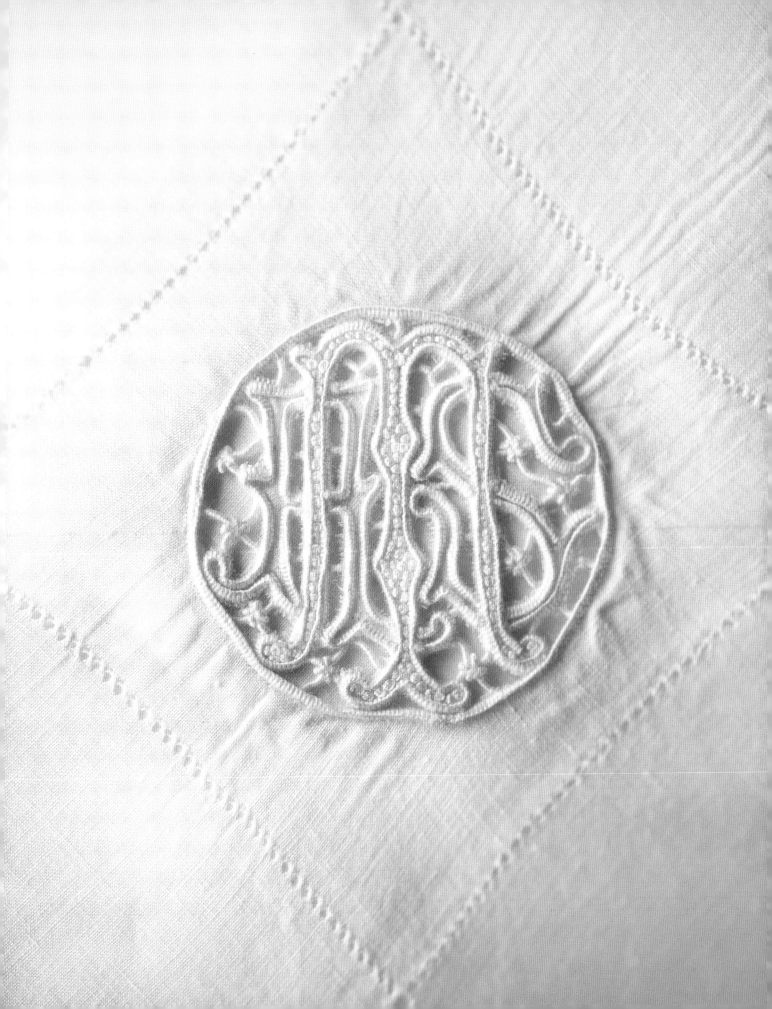

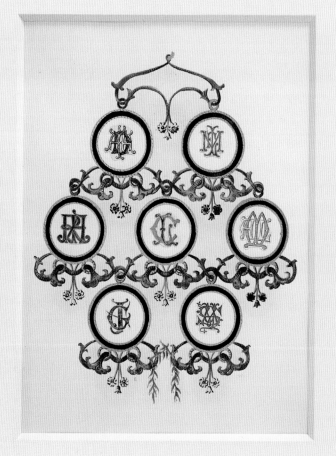

markings maintained their practical use to help the service providers keep their clients' valuables in order.

A major evolution of the monogram occurred as the French kings and their courts began to personalize their belongings with large crests, coats of arms and symbols that often included stylized letters. This was the start of the decorative use of monograms, as the embroidery was done in a flamboyant and not-so-discreet manner. The embellishments were fashionable and certainly served as confirmations of the owner's position and wealth. From their entrance gates to their floors and tiles, castles and chateaux were dripping in these early personal brand statements.

It didn't take long for this new trend to trickle down. Others followed what the royals were doing, and soon the monogram became a standard element on any fine linen or quality item for the home. As a woman married and put together her trousseau in the 1800s, the monogram became a rich symbol of her family's status. European society embraced the trend, and even the less-fortunate often had some sort of decorative family marking on their linens. Professional hand engraver Eric Margry shares that "by the 1800s, hand engraving was popular on many personal items. Monograms and messages were a way to personalize rings, watches, lockets, boxes, hand mirrors, hair brushes, flasks, cigarette cases." The engravings were so well done that many are still evident on antique pieces today.

During the Victorian era, monograms were at the pinnacle of their popularity. Monogram artists, such as Karl Klimsch, were applauded for their use of clean lines, shading and their new abilities to give a three-dimensional effect to the alphabet. The hobby of collecting monograms in scrapbooks began in the Victorian era, around 1860, about the same time that the envelope became standard in the post. Crest albums were published with beautifully designed pages, and collectors cut out the cyphers, crests and monograms from letters they received in the post and adhered them to the pages.

FINDING YOUR
Monogram Style

Finding your monogram style can be a great deal of fun! The options are endless, and you can use your imagination to combine styles and letters that are meaningful to you. With a little bit of imagination, you can create something that will represent your individual style. Are you drawn to simple clean lines, retro art deco looks or elaborate traditional designs?

Also consider the style of your home. Sometimes the most obvious choices are not the best. In a sleek modern home, the thin clean lines of an antique Victorian monogram might be the best way to add a decorative punch. Custom monogram artist Claudia Engle believes that "gender influences lettering choices as well. Block lettering has a more masculine feel and is, therefore, fitting for a male's monogram, while script lettering tends to be more feminine." She goes on to point out that "motifs or ornamentation that hold some personal significance for the individual can also be incorporated into the monogram." I love adding a personal motif to a monogram if the occasion calls for it. I especially love doing that for children or for a special event.

Research. Research. Research.—Always! The Internet is an incredible resource and you just may discover something entirely new to you.

—ALEX HITZ

Whatever your style, select something that can be printed, engraved or embroidered on all of the things you cherish at home. Thanks to technology, it is now more affordable than ever to make your mark on any of your favorite things. The affordability of monograms today has certainly not diminished our attraction to them.

Malia Dreyer of Lettermade is a namesake of her mother and grandmother. For this reason, her three-letter monogram holds an even deeper sentiment for her. She says, "I love traditional three-letter monograms; my first and middle name are both part of my mother's and grandmother's names as well; I love that every time I monogram my linens, generations before me are part of the embroidery."

You must pick a monogram that speaks to you. There are so many ways a monogram can reflect an individual—lettering, color, placement, frequency, etc. Pick hues and lettering that speak to your personality. If you want something different, play with the size and placement a bit.

—MARGRETTA WIKERT

Custom Monograms

The art of the custom monogram has been carried on by very few designers today. It is becoming more and more difficult to find an artist with a deep enough understanding of lettering that they can create beautiful custom cyphers on a truly one-of-a-kind level.

When our son was born, he ended up with five names on his birth certificate! It wasn't planned, but we left the hospital with a baby who might always have a hard time finding an easy monogram. I did a little bit of research and found Caroline Brackenridge, an artist in New York City who specialized in creative custom monograms. The process was really rewarding. I had a consultation on the phone with her about what the monogram would be used for and what styles we liked. She went to work and created six hand drawings for us to start with. I told her which parts of each drawing I liked and we carried on from there. It was such a treat to watch the process from start to finish, and I highly recommend following the same model when requesting your own custom monogram. Though Caroline doesn't seem to be working on new monograms anymore, I have found a new artist to work with on any future projects who works in much the same manner.

In selecting a monogram, strive to have it complement the personality and style of the owner. It should also be balanced in scale with the piece it will decorate.

—LYNN RUSSELL

Claudia Engle is the owner of Claudia Engle Lettering & Design. After an initial conversation about style and preferences, she goes to work hand drawing some samples for her clients. She describes the process:

With their preferences in mind, I provide the client with several preliminary sketches. From these sketches, they can continue to request revisions until the final design is complete. This is a collaborative effort, so I depend on and appreciate their input! Upon completion, I produce the camera-ready artwork necessary for reproduction. This artwork is provided to the client in a variety of file formats. I also provide instructional information as to how to go about executing the monogram on a variety of items.

—CLAUDIA ENGLE

When it comes to selecting a monogram, there are a few mistakes you want to avoid. Heather Wiese-Alexander of Bell'Invito says she has seen "unbalanced letters; graphic designers trying to take two letters from a typeface or calligraphy and force them together instead of drawing or re-designing the letters together so that they fit like a true unit. A monogram should appear as a single unit once it's finished, even if the letters are not joined." Another mistake might be that the letters are hard to make out. Alex Hitz believes that "with a monogram, you must, must, must be able to read the letters." There are times when the letters get so stylized that they are hard to see within the cypher. This can be especially tricky with certain letters, so rely on your designer to guide you.

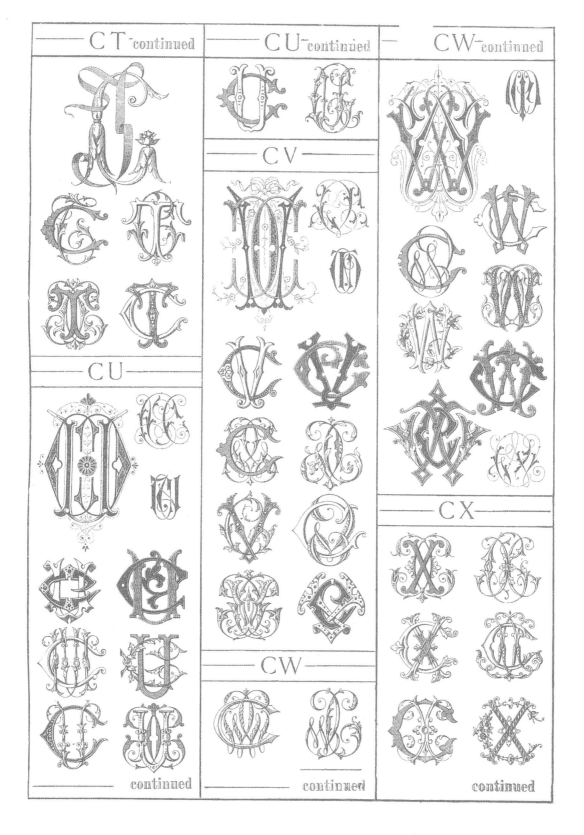

MONOGRAMS RESOURCES

I find great inspiration in the books of vintage monograms I have collected throughout the years. Some of my favorites are *The Encyclopedia of Monograms* by Leonard G. Lee and Dover publications, including *2,100 Victorian Monograms* by Karl Klimsch and *Treasury of Floral Designs and Initials for Artists and Craftspeople*, edited by Mary Carolyn Waldrep. These wonderful resources are filled with thousands of copyright-free monogram examples that are easy to reproduce. Maybe you will be lucky enough to find a design you love with your initials, or perhaps you will find inspiration for a custom design.

Vintage Monograms

Many people enjoy collecting antique or vintage monogrammed items. The quality of craftsmanship is amazing and, sadly, rarely matched today. Most collectors don't even mind if the monogram does not match their own initials; they love the graphic elements and decorative design of the custom work. From linens to silver, vintage and antique monogrammed items are in high demand.

Often times, single-letter monograms were used on linens because brides would have them in their trousseau before their marriages. Single initials were taken from their first names so they could continue to use the items after marriage. Silver was often gifted as a wedding or silver anniversary present, so most silver pieces have more than one-letter monograms. It was common practice to monogram silver before 1900, as it was very valuable and the monogram was placed there as a mark of ownership. Sadly, some monograms that were truly works of art have been removed from antique silver pieces because the letters did not match the new owners. Even some heirloom pieces have had monograms removed because a grandmother's name rarely matches that of a married granddaughter. I am of the thinking we should celebrate the monogram artist's work, whether the initials match ours or not.

When it comes to vintage linens, imagination is key. Be open to any initials and look for quality and beautiful design. Mismatched vintage monogrammed hand towels make wonderful napkins piled up on a buffet! Many style setters are now dyeing vintage linens from their white, cream or natural linen colors to bright and vivid shades that coordinate with their homes. This is a great trick for beautiful old linen that might otherwise be doomed due to a stubborn stain!

I use antique and vintage linens mixed with my more current things all the time. I adore vintage linens because you can get so much better quality and often something more unique than what is available today. I buy things with a monogram even if it is not mine, because I love the craftsmanship, tradition and values that things with a monogram represent to me.

—DANIELLE ROLLINS

Old-school rules
of traditional
points of view can
achieve integrity,
while use of color
may introduce
modernity.

— LYNN RUSSELL

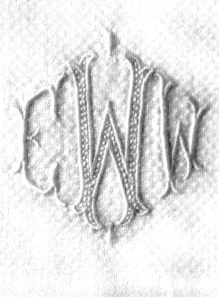

I think a monogram's personal style is represented in the colors chosen. A traditional monogram or crest that has been used for generations can take on a whole new modern "oomph" with the use or an updated or "funky" color combination.

—COURTLAND SMITH STEVENS

Monograms are their own artform regardless of simplicity or elaborate detail.

—LYNN RUSSELL

Monograms

AT HOME

We all know the importance of a first impression. A monogram at the front door can make an impact on your guests from the moment they arrive. In lieu of a wreath or holiday decoration, consider a monogram to complement the style of your home. From modern and sleek to regal or nautical, a laser-cut wooden monogram is a great accent for your home. I love the work that Authentic Monogram and Custom Art offers on Etsy. In order to make each monogram visually balanced and aesthetically pleasing, they do a lot of extra work to their orders. They may extend or reduce some parts of the letters to make the letters more readable and create the most well proportioned and beautiful monogram.

A pretty monogrammed tray on your entrance table can be a nice drop spot for keys and sunglasses and even a front hall coat closet can be enhanced with a monogram. Personalized coat hangers make a great first impression and work beautifully in a guest room as well. They would be a great gift for the friend who has everything!

Monograms are used most often as a means to add a special decorative touch to the table. They are a subtle way to add color and accent beautiful china and flowers. I hope these exquisite examples of table details will inspire you to take your linens straight to your monogrammer! Whether it is the linens, place cards, menu cards or your silver, a monogram can personalize the style of your table and make an impact on your guests.

One of my favorite ways to elevate my table settings is with monogrammed napkins, which I have been collecting since I got married. The monograms not only add a punch of color but also make those who use them feel special and important. Some of my linen napkins are special heirloom-quality pieces, but most of them are very inexpensive linens to which I have added a touch of embroidery.

Nalorie

Barbara

Margaret

Elizabeth

Kimberly

Menu

Soupe du Jour

La Salade de Crabe et Avocat

Les Poissons
Branzino avec des Petits Légumes
Pan-Seared Mediterranean Sea Bass
with Mixed Vegetables, Melted Leeks,
and Shallot Vinaigrette

— OR —

et Les Viandes
Filet de Boeuf Grillé, Sauce au Poivre
Grilled Filet Mignon, Pomme Purée,
Grilled Asparagus, Rainbow Baby Carrots,
and Peppercorn Sauce

Profiteroles and Mixed Berries
Cognac Sauce with Chantilly Cream

In a world that is increasingly overrun with the marketing of corporate images, it is important to remember that a monogram is a personal "logo" and deserves the same attention to good design. Creating a symbol for yourself, or for someone else if you are in the business of monogramming, can be a very rewarding process.

—ALEXA PULITZER

On the tabletop, engraved silverware, napkin rings and embroidered napkins add a lot of oomph. And in years to come, these heirloom pieces pass on to the next generation, still carrying your mark.

—MA ALLEN

I like to work with clients on using elements that are important to their personal style, family heritage or geographic location. All of those elements can be incorporated with the letters to create a one-of-a-kind look for their monogram.

—EMILY MCCARTHY

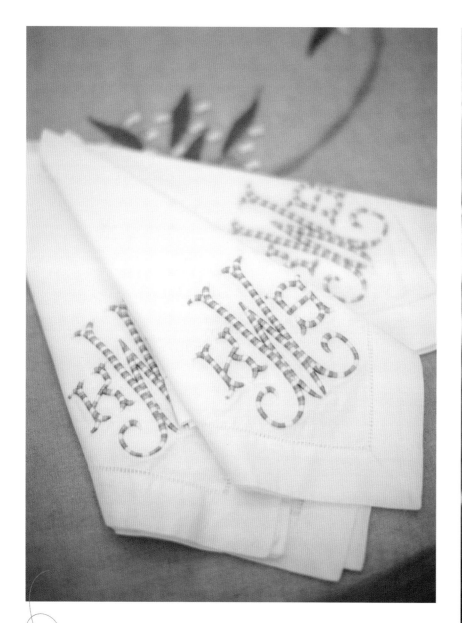

Mix traditional monograms with modern colors.

—KIRSTEN FITZGIBBONS &
KELLI FORD OF KIRSTENKELLI

When my husband and I got married, his mother gave us her wedding silver as a gift. It includes a W monogram that I have carried through to so many of our other things. I love it because it is classic and simple. I asked an embroidery artist to digitize the monogram for me so that I could have it added to other items. Once the monogram was digital, I could add it to almost anything! I used it for stationery, linen napkins, and other pieces of silver. It is very satisfying to be able to carry on something so beautiful in our house that my husband enjoyed in his childhood.

When choosing a monogram for your table, carefully consider the way you like to entertain. We like to host all types of parties, from laid-back buffets to formal seated dinners, so I was thrilled that the monogram passed down to me by my stylish mother-in-law was so versatile. It can look formal and traditional and modern all at the same

NAPKIN MONOGRAMS

When adding a monogram to a napkin, place and orient it toward the left corner of the napkin. This way, regardless of whether you fold it in a triangle or a rectangle, the monogram will still show. When selecting the placement of a monogram on a placemat, you have several choices. Anything around the edge of the placemat, from the upper left corner to the center top, will leave the monogram exposed throughout a meal; but for a fun surprise consider a large monogram in the center of the placemat, so that when a plate is lifted the design is revealed. I use my monogrammed linens for every occasion, from takeout at home to formal dinner parties. I love Summer Tompkins Walker's suggestion that "an embroidered monogram on a napkin can change the tone of your table according to the season."

time. It was gifted to me on silver flatware and I added it to the napkins we used at our wedding dinner. I still use our wedding napkins today, so the investment was certainly worthwhile!

It's nice to have napkins for seasonal parties. Invest in some that are dressy for holidays and more formal parties and get creative with fresh and light designs for spring and summer parties. If you're concerned about size and placement, Tompkins Walker assures us that "when it comes to napkins, the bigger the monogram the better. It is so nice to have luxurious and oversized napkins. Napkins make the place setting. Most people will never notice the plates but they will always remember the special napkins."

As lovely a touch and versatile as napkins can be, monogrammed silver, particularly heirloom pieces, are perhaps more cherished. Anything from flatware to silver cups can carry a monogram and provide great conversation starters at a dinner party. Monogrammed silver cups can be used for drinks or for flowers. I love to place mix-and-match monogrammed cups filled with flowers around the table or buffet for smaller pops of color. However you use it, let the monograms stand as understated statements of your personal style or as homage to your ancestors. Celebrate and honor them by using their beautiful items often.

Vintage silver napkin rings are also often found on the table again today. They are rich with tradition and were often given as baby gifts and marked a new family member's seat at every meal. They are highly collectable and often copied by new manufacturers.

Monogrammed porcelain is less common but certainly just as special as silver. Brides are adding it to their registries more and more frequently. Current brands, such as Pickard and Raynaud, are offering them more frequently, and vintage sets are found from time to time. The vintage sets are typically very elaborate and often include a coat of arms or family crest with a monogram. George Vanderbilt monogrammed almost everything he possibly could at Biltmore, the largest house in America, and that included all of the china services. It is certainly a grand gesture, but a beautiful one as well.

Glassware and crystal are not often found with a monogram either but it can be a beautiful way to add a unique design to something that is found at every table. Respectable fine crystal lines such as Moser and Royal Brierley are offering monogram services on many of their styles for bridal registries, a sure sign that the monogram is back in style for the table.

The Powder Room

The powder room is the perfect place to add a personal touch with a monogram. Fingertip towels are the easiest way. I like to collect vintage towels with W monograms on them and stack them beside the sink when I have a party. I also have disposable linen-like hand towels with an elaborate monogram. Even though they are disposable, they are elevated up a notch in style with the addition of the monogram.

Monograms can be added to both the simple and the special items in your powder room. In addition to linens, monogrammed items such as a small hand mirror or a box with a sewing kit and stain pen for your guests to use, can be added to a powder room. Both add pretty decorative elements that also show forethought in predicting your guests' needs.

In addition to these practical items, a monogrammed candle can warm a powder room and a small monogrammed cup can hold flowers. Depending on how far you want to go, you can even find monogrammed soaps and toilet paper rolls these days!

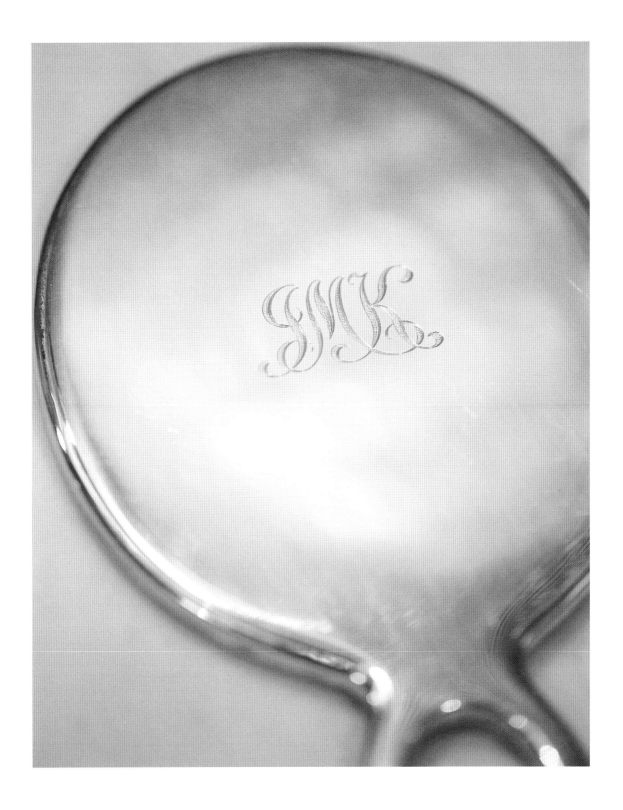

Monograms tell a story about traditions, family
history, namesakes, and express personal taste and
style.

—MALIA DREYER

The Bedroom

Monograms are best used as a personal proclamation on the linens of a bedroom. A bedroom is a sanctuary designed to provide comfort and rest. There is a soothing quality to a beautifully designed bed covered in luxurious linens; but even if your budget doesn't call for the finest quality sheets, adding a personal touch such as an embroidered monogram can elevate your bedding. Alexa Pulitzer suggests that they key to the perfect monogrammed bed linens is to "think oversized, particularly if you have a king-size bed."

In a shared bedroom, a monogram can help a child make their own mark and give them a sense of ownership over their own space. In a room with two beds, complementary linens can be distinguished by adding the personal touch of a monogram to each.

For bedside tables, a monogrammed cup, box or tray makes a great spot to collect trinkets and jewelry, or can be used to add a little life to the room by holding fresh flowers. I keep a pretty decoupage monogram tray from Kelly Wilson Antiques on my bedside table. It cannot be used for food service, as it is so delicate, but it is a pretty reminder of the friend who gave it to me as a gift and a nice complement to the blue and white bed linens next to it.

Monograms are an aesthetic complement to an object, be it linen, porcelain, glass, paper or silver.

—LYNN RUSSELL

EMBROIDERY

With embroidery, a monogram is stitched onto the fabric with thread.
It is dainty and delicate, and very thin lines can be embroidered
within a design. There are four basic types of stitches: outline, border,
detached and filling. Embroidery by hand is rare and very special. Several
companies still offer hand embroidery, and machine embroidery services
are very easy to find. Most tailors offer machine embroidery.

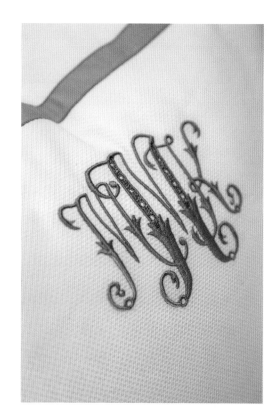

A monogram is that endearing visual footprint that not only links generations, but is a unique stamp of personality in your home. Whether classic or with a modern twist, those letters become more than just letters . . . they are the gracious, finishing touch of YOU.

—KELLY WILSON

Monograms can be used in a multitude of ways in the bathroom. The list of vanity items that can benefit from a personal mark is long. From towels to cosmetics bags, the bath is a popular spot for personalization. This goes to show that a monogram is no longer simply an expression of power and status, but a personal touch that can make life's simplest everyday tasks feel a little bit more luxurious.

They can also be practical, though. If a family or siblings share a bathroom, monograms can be a wonderful way to distinguish belongings. For towels and bathroom linens, it is a stylish way to mark ownership. Monogrammed cosmetics bags can help keep a shared bathroom's toiletries organized, and valet trays can help keep cuff links and jewelry in the right hands.

For the gentlemen, a leather valet tray with a monogram in the corner, or a Lucite tray to hold keys and pocket change can add personalized touches to decorate their space. I love the valet trays and masculine boxes offered by Mark & Graham. The looks are simple and traditional but with a distinguished modern flare.

In a world where everything is readily available and mass-produced, a monogram is still one of a kind.

— COURTLAND SMITH STEVENS

APPLIQUÉ

Appliqué is a French term that refers to the sewing technique where one piece of fabric is applied to another and sewn on. This technique typically combines two different textures and works well on a broader monogram. Almost any fabric can be used for the appliqué and allows for play with patterns and colors.

There are so many fun ways to incorporate a monogram into your kitchen. From customized recipe cards to cutting boards, the mark of your signature style can be carried through in a more playful and colorful way in the kitchen. Disposable or easily replaceable items are a great way to bring a bit of cheerful color and fun motifs into play in your home. When you are not engraving an heirloom, loosen the reigns and try styles and motifs that might not normally be your cup of tea!

Other fun ways to add a personalized touch to the kitchen include scratch pads by the telephone or a monogrammed dish by the sink to hold your rings. These are fun and inexpensive ways to add detail to a room that we spend so much of our time in.

I adore hand-stitched monograms, but I think machine done can look lovely too. Regardless of which one you choose, the back should look as pretty as the front if it is real quality.

— DANIELLE ROLLINS

Go with your gut and order what jumps out at you. Vacillating and second-guessing usually result in forever questioning your decision. Don't labor over your decision. Have fun with it and don't take it too seriously.

—MARGRETTA WIKERT

The Bar

n most households, the barware is the gentleman's territory. Because of that, it traditionally holds the man's monogram. It is an area that easily lends itself to personal expression and is a nice place to have the gentleman of the house use his own classic mark.

Monogrammed cocktail napkins make the perfect hostess gift! Gifting a hostess personalized linen napkins not only shows gratitude, but forethought and appreciation. A cocktail party is that much more elegant with a little bit of tradition and monogrammed linens.

—MALIA DREYER, *LETTERMADE*

Bar items should suit the personal style of the owner. Modernity can be effective through use of unexpected colors.

—LYNN RUSSELL

Though one can't deny the ease of email, there is something slightly thrilling about finding a good, old-fashioned personal note in the mail, especially one that is stamped with the sender's monogram. Today's paper trends are inspired by examples of beautiful old papers monogrammed in traditional styles. Long-standing American companies, such as The Printery, are using vibrant colors and custom monograms adapted from their traditional collections to create exciting new stationery wardrobes for today's discerning note writers.

Etiquette expert Peggy Post believes that keeping the tools that you need to write thank-you notes handy is important. I keep my monogrammed note cards in a silver toast rack on my desk as a reminder to write a note to someone I am grateful for each day. Alexa Pulitzer has created a beautiful brand of monogrammed goods combining classic motifs and lettering. When it comes to note cards and paper goods, she recommends placing a monogram in the top left, middle left or centered on the top. "Once you have selected a beautiful monogram that represents your personal style, invest in having a plate made to engrave your mark into paper goods. You can play around with placement and colors every time you re-order your items," says Pulitzer.

In addition to stationery, you might consider some other monogrammed accents for your work area. Kirsten and Kelli suggest "a tissue box cover, which is always so pretty on the desk, with a monogram. We also love a luxurious throw in the home office."

Interior designer MA Allen suggests bringing in some monogrammed silver to personalize your desktop. Instead of an office-grade container, monogrammed trays are great for corralling all the odds and ends needed on a desk."

As William James wrote, 'There is no immaculate conception of ideas.' I believe most creative endeavors are sparked by the things we find resonate with us. To this end, in picking a monogram, I always advise people to survey their personal landscape for the things they're drawn to. This usually leads us to what they like in a monogram.

—WILLIAM MILLER OF *THE PRINTERY*

'm so enamored with monograms that I selected my baby's name so that she shared my monogram! Bonnets, crib sheets and diaper bags are not the only things that have been branded for baby lately. So many baby items, already precious in their own right, have been personalized with a monogram. Traditionally, babies would not have a monogram of their own but their items would instead be embroidered with their first names only. However, the trend today leans towards using monograms in a decorative way for baby. Whether on the crib valence or a pillow in the nursery, baby monograms are widely enjoyed and the old-school rules are tossed out with the dirty diapers. Today's parents are having fun creating a monogram that is a perfect fit for their little bundles of love and joy. For items that are bound to become heirloom pieces, such as silver cups or bowls, a monogram is meaningful and adds a personalized touch to baby's items.

When choosing nursery décor, consider a monogram on pieces that can last in the little one's room as it changes with growth. For a client's first baby, designer Amy Berry helped the couple select specific items to monogram based on whether the items would stay in the child's room long-term. She said they "used the same monogram in the crib valance and with the towels, since both were things that would grow with her. That valance will probably hang over a daybed one day. The client actually ended up using the same monogram on her stationary too! The monograms made everything so special."

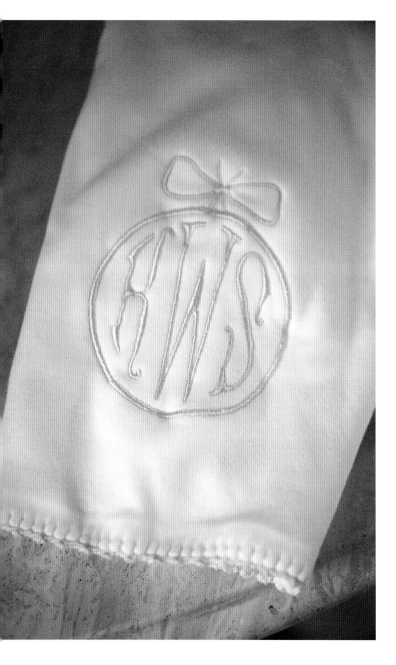

The living room is a wonderful place to add elegant touches with a monogram. Whether it is a colorful throw pillow placed to add a splash of color to a neutral sofa or a slipcover for a chair, these classic touches can really personalize your space. Even lampshades can carry a monogram.

Whether you favor classic and traditional or hip and edgy, your custom initials logo can give your living room panache.

Monograms are so incredibly telling—the bold and flowery ones are for confident, ornate types, while the geometric ones tell a more understated story. The plainest ones, with just block letters and periods seem to be the most austere, the most powerful.

— ALEX HITZ

I love monograms, from engraved to embroidered to layered appliqués. There are so many unique styles outside of the standard-issue monogram that has become widespread. I love looking back at old family crests, royal signatures and Victorian monograms for inspiration. A modern take on the monogram using unexpected typography and colors makes for a fun personalization of really anything you can come up with. From a practical solution, the monogram today can be one's brand, and who doesn't love good branding, right?

— MA ALLEN, INTERIOR DESIGNER

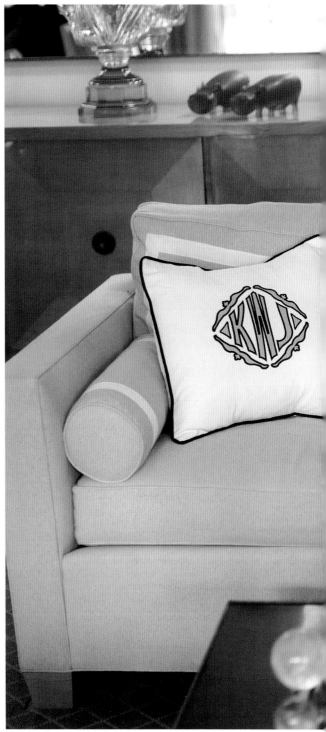

My cousin has an old chair carved with the Wiese family inscription that dates back several generations. From the moment I saw it, I coveted that chair. Not because of any monetary value, but because it had a mark that made it personal. Monograms are not only a beautiful statement of personal taste, they add a tangible piece of humanity to every object they adorn. An heirloom monogram, when properly employed, serves as a personal mark for a person or family for many years. In today's terms, it is a personal brand identity. Once that brand is established, the value of the monogram is indelible to the brand followers, who may be millions of adoring fans, or a few cherished heirs.

—HEATHER WIESE-ALEXANDER, BELL'INVITO

The Holidays

Winter is the most festive time of the year and I love to decorate and entertain with classic monogram decorations. There are many ways to personalize your home around the holidays with monograms. From a mono-
gram wreath to a set of stockings, the possibilities seem endless. Even giftwrap, tags
and ribbon are often found with a monogram customization. This classic tradition is a
great way to honor family and friends. In addition, as Kirsten and Kelli point out, "As
a gift, an item with a monogram is much more thoughtful."

The holidays are another opportunity to grace your table with festive monograms.
Beautiful monograms on a napkin can be embellished with embroidered holiday
motifs such as fir and pinecones or candy canes. Even simply selecting a red thread for
your monogram's embroidery on a white linen napkin can add a merry touch to your
holiday table.

B·R·L

FROM

Blair Locke

To me, monograms tell a story of history and style through the ages. They are festive and chic. They celebrate occasions. They chart passages and life events. I am addicted to monograms.

—ALEX HITZ

Monograms are unique to you and your family; therefore, they should reflect your style and family heritage. They become an insignia for use around your home and to unofficially brand your home.

—EMILY MCCARTHY

Monogram Etiquette

There are some simple rules of etiquette for monogram designs that can help ensure that you have all of the letters in the right place! Before you begin to make your mark, read through the following pages to make sure you are comfortable with the traditions. Now, that said, there are many who believe that monograms are works of art in which rules are not meant to be followed. When I asked Alex Hitz how he felt about monogram rules, he said, "Now, Kim, you know just as well as I do that rules are made to be broken. But you must learn them before you break them."

Summer Tompkins Walker agrees, saying, "Monograms reflect you, so be yourself in choosing and listen to your inner voice."

If you are playing with a unique way of combining letters and varied letter styles, layers upon layers of letters can be twisted and turned together to create a beautiful cypher that might not need an order.

Other people throw the rules of order for monogramming away if their letters spell something distasteful. For example, if your name were Patrick Ian Gleason, you wouldn't want PIG pasted over the towels you see first thing each morning! Instead, you might opt for a double-letter monogram or unique custom cypher. Don't worry if your initials are less than perfect in a row. You can simply use only first and last initials for a two-letter monogram or rearrange the letters in an order that does work for you. Even the finest royals have this issue sometimes: Prince William and Catherine, Duchess of Cambridge have broken with centuries of royal tradition and separated their letters in their duogram, as WC is the standard marking for water closet in Europe!

When ordering a stock monogram item, be sure to ask for a proof so that you can see how the monogram looks with your initials. Some letters are easier to incorporate

into a design than others. Monogram experts seem to unanimously agree that the most beautiful letters in a monogram are M, W, B, E, A, and S. If you are carrying a J, I, F, or L initial, I'm sorry to say that they are the hardest! Courtland Smith Stevens and her team at Number Four Eleven agree and point out that P and T can be tough letters as well. Search for a type style that makes these letters easy to make out. Whatever your initials, don't hesitate to turn to the professionals for design advice. Their experience with different styles and lettering can help you find the perfect fit for you.

Peggy Post believes that there is "a good merger of both the traditional rules and great design in today's monograms. Bending traditions as it makes sense is fine as long as it doesn't offend anyone." I couldn't agree more! The key point, as Peggy Post points out, is that "people feel strongly about their names and their initials are very personal." Traditions and rules are in place to make people secure and confident, but anyone who wants or needs to bend them a bit should feel comfortable doing so as long as it doesn't come at anyone else's expense.

My favorite "rule" is that there really are no "rules!" Technically, the rules of etiquette apply to monogram design, but if the monogram is going to be reflective of the individual it needs to include elements the client is comfortable with. For example, if a married female chooses to use her middle name rather than her maiden name in the monogram, she should be entitled to do so. Quite often, an individual is called by his middle name rather than his first name. If that is the case, I would recommend that the middle name initial be used. A monogram is a mark of identity and needs to be true to the individual!

—CLAUDIA ENGLE, MONOGRAM ARTIST

TRADITIONAL MONOGRAM ETIQUETTE

Bedroom Linens: Traditionally, bedroom linens feature the monogram of the lady of the house; however, today a couple's duogram is perfectly appropriate. Many gentlemen feel that they share the bed and should be represented as well.

Barware: According to old-school rules, a gentleman's monogram should grace the barware. This is because it was customary for the men and women to retreat to separate areas of the house after a meal or get-together. Today, that has changed, but the man's monogram on barware continues to be the most popular choice.

Regarding the rules of barware, Jill Giddens and Anne Marie Goodwin of Me & Re Design give this advice: "While we respect the old-school man's monogram on barware, we also love to mix it up! When it's an heirloom piece, like a silver tray, stick to traditional monogram rules, but for disposable items, like Styrofoam cups, anything goes."

Bar linens might be a different story, though. Large cocktail napkins are elegant and perfect for a monogram. Consider what Courtland Smith Stevens from Number Four Eleven suggests: "A 4 x 6 fold-over cocktail napkin seems to be in demand these days. It gives you more options for embroidery. You can do the monogram large in the center along the hemstitch or smaller in the lower right-hand corner. On a 6 x 6 cocktail napkin, we most often place the monogram dead center. It looks beautiful, but try to balance a wine glass on a huge raised monogram. I always suggest putting it small in the right-hand corner."

Bath: Bath linens should be monogrammed with the user's initials. If a bathroom is shared among family members, this is a great way to designate which linens belong to each person. If the linen is for a guest powder room, select either a single letter monogram of the homeowner's last name or use the monogram of the lady of the house.

Table Linens: The lady's monogram is traditionally used for table linens, but for a fun or festive approach, consider using a fun and applicable three-letter word, such as YUM or EAT!

Knowing when and where to properly use a monogram is a beautiful layer of polish that not many in the modern era possess. I'm an old-school girl with modern sensibilities, so having said that, I can also be all for breaking the rules. The key here is that you have to know a rule to break it (well). For example, when entertaining, it's traditional that a woman's monogram, either a mark with her maiden pedigree or a monogram with her married initial, would be used atop of a dinner menu. Why? Simply, women were in charge of the social aspects of the home. Today, when a couple is hosting a dinner that might be accented with a printed menu, a monogram for the couple would more likely be used. I have a good friend whose career is such that her husband has chosen to be the domestic dynamic. I've often wondered, how correct—and courageous—would it be for him to use his monogram in the placement of what would have traditionally been hers?

—HEATHER WIESE-ALEXANDER

Heirlooms: There is such a special meaning in using an inherited monogrammed item. I feel so blessed to be able to entertain with some pieces that were passed down to me. Even if we have some pieces with different initials on them, it is perfectly okay to use them without apology. Peggy Post enjoys using some cherished family silver engraved with a family letter G.

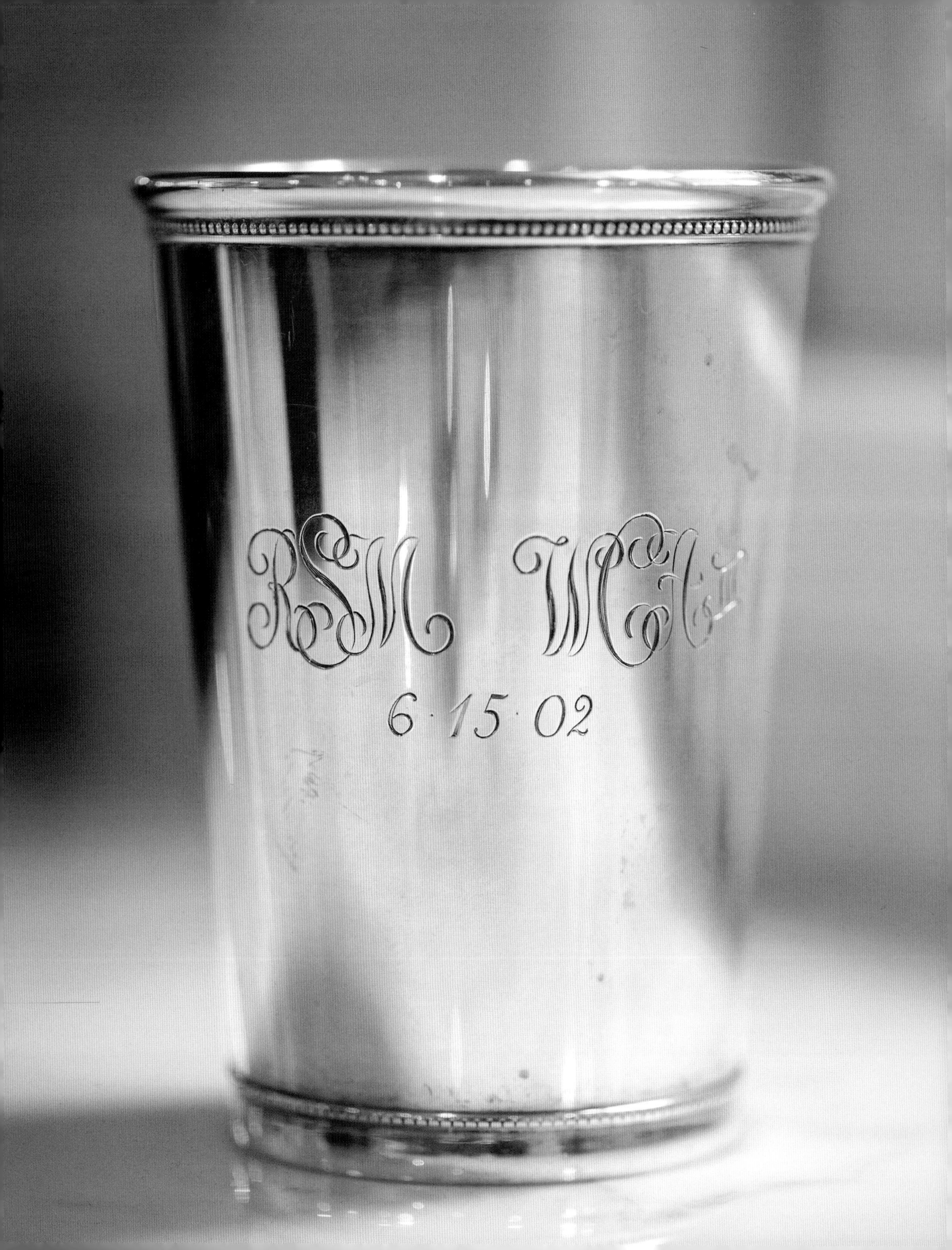
6·15·02

ACCORDING TO MARITAL STATUS

SINGLE FEMALE
First LAST Middle, with the middle initial larger than the flanking initials.
Example: Kimberly Jayne Schlegel = kSj

MARRIED FEMALE
First LAST Maiden, with the middle initial larger than the flanking initials.
Example: Kimberly Schlegel Whitman = kWs

SINGLE OR MARRIED MALE
First Middle Last, with all initials being the same size
Example: James Robert Whitman = JRW

MARRIED COUPLES
Traditionally, as monogram expert Margretta Wikert points out, "a monogram is just that, mono, which means self!" I'm all for traditional rules, but not everyone thinks they are still applicable today. Creating a duogram is an example of a time when it's fine to break the rules! I believe that a monogram is first and foremost a visual marking, so selecting the letters that are most visually pleasing is perfectly acceptable. If that means including another's initials, so be it. Summer Tompkins Walker agrees. She thinks, "in a world where women and men are becoming equals, it is nice to incorporate the man into the initials and not use only women's initials." If you are combining the letters of two people's names, it is referred to as a duogram. If you do want to create a duogram, remember the "ladies first" rule and place the initial of her first name in the first space. Use the lady's first initial, Married Last Name in the center, and the husband's first initial.

Example: Kimberly and Justin Whitman = kWj

ENGAGED COUPLES

Custom monogram artist Claudia Engle recommends a duogram incorporating the couple's first name initials only. She says, "when designing a monogram for an engaged couple, I begin with the joint monogram design and simply 'lift' the duogram from it. This insures a consistent look in regard to both monograms." It is not appropriate for an engaged couple to use a combined cypher before their wedding ceremony. Once they have completed the ceremony, they may use their combined initials.

DIVORCE

What should you do with your monogrammed items after a divorce? I turned to Peggy Post, great-grand-daughter-in-law of etiquette expert Emily Post, for advice on this question. She says, "as long as the new husband doesn't have a problem with it, why not continue to use it or give it as a gift to one of the children from the first marriage? It would be a shame for your beautiful monogrammed silver or porcelain to go unused."

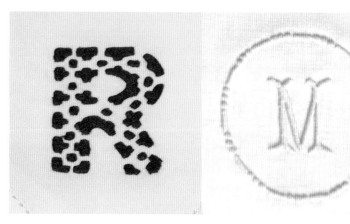

SINGLE-LETTER MONOGRAMS

Monograms for unmarried people are often the first-name initial, allowing for the addition of surname initials at a later time. Single-letter monograms are prime for additional design embellishments.

TWO-LETTER MONOGRAMS

Place the letters in FIRST/LAST order or intertwine them to create a cypher.

THREE LETTER MONOGRAMS

If all three letters are the same size, they should go in FIRST/MIDDLE/LAST order. If the center letter is larger, the letters should go in FIRST/LAST/MIDDLE order.

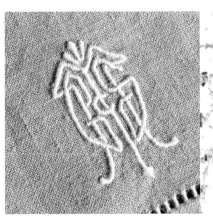

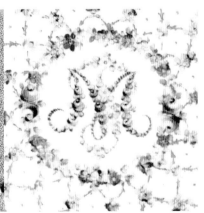

MORE THAN THREE-LETTER MONOGRAMS

Consider listing them in order or creating a cypher (an elaborate design in which the monogram is secretly encoded).

Acknowledgments

Thank you to Mason and Allen Custard, Kelli and Jerry Ford, Myrna and Robert Schlegel, Krystal Schlegel, Kari and Troy Kloewer, Robert Keeley, Lynn Russell, Natalie and Mike McGuire, and Lana and Barry Andrews for allowing me to invade your homes and dig through your amazing collections of monogrammed treasures for our photographs.

Special thanks to Hannah Ferguson and Cynthia Nouri of Sasha Nicholas, Malia Dreyer of Lettermade, Courtland Smith Stevens of Number Four Eleven, Summer Tompkins Walker of Walker Valentine Custom House, Danielle Rollins, Alex Hitz, Sharyn Blond, Julia Berger of Julia B., Margretta Wikert of Ellis Hill, Alexa Pulitzer, MA Allen, Kirsten Fitzgibbons and Kelli Ford of KirstenKelli LLC, Madison, Jen O'Neal, Kelly Wilson, William Miller of The Printery, Heather Wiese-Alexander of Bell'Invito, Suzanne Droese and Lauren Millet and the Droese Team, Todd Fiscus, Claudia Engle, Jill Giddens and Anne Marie Goodwin of Me & Re Design, Cynthia Smoot, Peggy Post, Eric Margry, David Desmond, Michelle Lockhart of Charlotte Max, Paula Minnis of Gaia for Women, Michele Chisholm of Calico Daisy Handmade, and Emily McCarthy for lending their Monogram Expertise.

To my family, Justin, JR and Millie Stuart, thank you for letting me turn our home into a photo studio and putting up with my messes! To my parents, thank you for all that you do to help every single day! You are the best!!!! I could not have pulled this together with out the help of my mother-in-law, Caroline Whitman, Kathy Short, Michael Bentley, and my supportive family and friends.

Big thanks to Kari Stuart at ICM and my wonderful editor, Madge Baird, who, after seven books with me, continues to have the patience to fix my work and consider my ideas! John Cain Sargent and Dan Arnold deserve an extra special Thank You for always keeping smiles on your faces even from behind the camera!

Resources

CUSTOM MONOGRAM DESIGN:

5 BY 7 DESIGNS
214.538.2800
www.5by7designs.com
annie@5by7designs.com

BELL'INVITO
214.741.1717
www.bellinvito.com

CLAUDIA ENGLE
859.806.2114
www.cengledesigns.com

EMILY J. MCCARTHY
912.856.2707
www.emilymccarthy.com

STATIONERY:

ALEXA PULITZER
504.945.4843
www.AlexaPulitzer.com

MINNIE & EMMA
1.800.521.0766
www.minnieandemma.com

THE PRINTERY
516.922.3250
www.iprintery.com

HOME ACCENTS:

AUTHENTIC MONOGRAM AND CUSTOM ART
www.etsy.com/shop/MonogramCustomArt

CALICO DAISY
www.etsy.com/shop/calicodaisy

CHARLOTTE MAX DESIGNS
www.CharlotteMax.com

ELLIS HILL
214.520.6108
www.ellis-hill.com

GAIA
858.200.5938
www.gaiaforwomen.com

KELLY WILSON ANTIQUES
www.kellywilsonantiques.com

MADISON
214.528.8118
www.Madison214.com

MARK & GRAHAM
www.markandgraham.com

MARY MCLAUGHLIN DESIGNS
844.446.6861
www.glazeware.com

ME & RE DESIGNS
www.meandredesign.com

NUMBER FOUR ELEVEN
912.443.0065
www.numberfoureleven.com

LINENS:

ELLIS HILL
214.520.6108
www.ellis-hill.com

HALO STUDIO
214.676.8717
www.halostudiogifts.com

JULIA B.
www.juliab.com

LETTERMADE
www.shoplettermade.com

LEONTINE LINENS
800.876.4799
www.leontinelinens.com

MADISON
214.528.8118
www.Madison214.com

MARK & GRAHAM
www.markandgraham.com

NUMBER FOUR ELEVEN
912.443.0065
www.numberfoureleven.com

SHARYN BLOND LINENS
913.362.4420
www.sharynblondlinens.com

WALKER VALENTINE CUSTOM HOUSE
415.265.9030
walkervalentine.com

ENGRAVING:

ERIC MARGRY FINE HAND ENGRAVING
703.548.7808
Alexandria, VA

PORCELAIN AND GLASS:

JACQUELINE POIRIER
www.jacquelinepoirier.com

JOY DE ROHAN CHABOT
www.joyderohanchabot.com

SASHA NICHOLAS
sashanicholas.com

INTERIOR DESIGN:

AMY BERRY DESIGN
214.288.9926
www.amyberrydesign.com

DANIELLE ROLLINS
404.944.2454
Rollins Ingram Design Architecture Gardens Lifestyle

JANET RICE INTERIORS
214.563.1935
www.janetriceinteriors.com

KIRSTEN KELLI LLC
www.kirstenkelli.com

LAURA LEE CLARK INTERIOR DESIGN, INC
214.265.7272
lauraleeclark.com

MA ALLEN INTERIORS
919.699.3131
www.maalleninteriors.com

ANTIQUES:

COPPER LAMP
214.369.5166
www.copperlamp.com

LYNN RUSSELL ANTIQUES
LynnRussellAntiques.com

Sources

PAGES 108/109: Kirsten Kelli Interior Design.

PAGE 110: Kirsten Kelli Interior Design.

PAGE 111: Applique towel, Calico Daisy handmade.

PAGE 112/113: Leontine Linens. Interior design, Laura Lee Clark.

PAGE 114: Leontine Linens. Interior design, Laura Lee Clark.

PAGE 115: Left, Leontine Linens, right, Sharyn Blond Linens.

PAGE 116/117: Leontine Linens. Interior design, Laura Lee Clark.

PAGE 118: Jewelry cases, Walker Valentine Custom House.

PAGE 119: Mark and Graham valet case.

PAGE 121: MA Allen Interiors.

PAGE 122: Cutting board by Me and Re Design.

PAGE 123: Mushroom monograms by Madison Dallas.

PAGE 125: Cocktail napkins by Mark and Graham.

PAGE 126: Cocktail napkin by Halo Home, hand-painted glass from Dior, navy painted tray from Wisteria.

PAGE 127: Cocktail napkin and wooden stir stick by Emily McCarthy.

PAGE 128: Fish cocktail napkins by Julia B., paper coasters by Emily McCarthy.

PAGE 129: Paper napkins by Emily McCarthy.

PAGE 130: Custom monogram by Claudia Engle.

PAGE 131: Hand towel by Madison, Dallas.

PAGE 133: Wastebasket by Charlotte Max. Desk from Jan Showers and Assoc.

PAGE 134/135: Vintage silver box, private collection. Custom silver box, Lolly Harrison at Stanley Korshak.

PAGE 136: Antique books, private collection, notepad by Alexa Pulitzer, pewter cup, antique.

PAGE 137: Notepad, Haute Papier.

PAGE 138/139: Notepads and stationery, Emily McCarthy.

PAGE 141: Pink and white monogram pillow, Ellis Hill. White monogram pillow made from vintage French linens.

PAGE 142: White cloth from Pixie Lily and monogram silver brush, Tiffany & Co.

PAGE 143: Quilted blanket, Leontine Linens.

PAGE 144/145: Amy Berry Interior Design.

PAGE 147: Applique pillow by Calico Daisy handmade.

PAGES 148/149: Kirsten Kelli Interior Design.

PAGE 150: Custom shade made from an antique monogram linen.

PAGE 151: Monogram slip covers by Beverly Field Interiors.

PAGE 152/153: Pillows from Madison, Dallas, photograph by Gray Malin.

PAGE 154/155: Applique pillows by Calico Daisy handmade.

PAGE 156: Pillow, Me & Re Design, blanket, Hermes.

PAGE 157: Tissue cover, Madison, Dallas.

PAGE 159: Stockings, Gaia for Women. Fireplace screen by Claire Crowe.

PAGES 160/161: Gift tags, Emily McCarthy.

PAGE 162: Monogram napkin by Madison, Dallas.

PAGE 163: Ornaments by Halo Home.

PAGE 164: Candy cane monogram by Madison, Dallas, plate, Grenadiers by Bernardaud.

PAGE 165: Sharyn Blond Linens.

PAGE 166: White linen napkin, vintage.

PAGE 169: Julia B. at Ellis Hill.

PAGE 171: Leontine Linens.

PAGE 173: Madison, Dallas.

PAGE 174: Madison, Dallas.

PAGE 175: Julia B. at Ellis Hill.

PAGE 177: All from Julia B. at Ellis Hill.

PAGES 178-183: Vintage monogrammed silver from private collections.

PAGE 182: Silver cup by Tiffany & Co.

PAGE 183: Engraving by Tiffany & Co, napkin by Julia B at Ellis Hill.

PAGE 184: Custom monogram, Claudia Engle; silver, vintage from private collection; R from Danielle Rollins, Leontine Linens "Rollins" monogram; M from Julia B. at Ellis Hill.

PAGE 185: Vintage gold-plated box, private collection.

PAGE 186: Hand-engraved silver plate, private collection.

PAGE 187: Linens, Julia B. at Ellis Hill. Bottom right, antique porcelain plate, private collection.

PAGE 189: Monogram cuff by Hannah Ferguson Jewelry.

PHOTO CREDITS

DAN ARNOLD: 33, 34, 35, 36, 37, 38, 39, 40, 41

QUENTIN BACON: 130, 184 top

CYNTHIA NOURI/STYLING BY REGINA ALONSO: 26, 49, 59, 69

PHILIP ESPARZA: 90

JOHN KERNICK: 56, 66, 184 lower left

JOHN CAIN SARGENT: 2, 6, 9, 12, 15, 18, 21, 22, 42, 45, 46, 47, 50, 51, 52, 53, 54, 55, 57, 58, 60, 61, 62, 63, 64, 65, 67, 68, 70, 71, 73, 74, 76, 77, 79, 80, 81, 82, 83, 84, 85, 86, 87, 89, 92, 93, 94, 95, 96, 98, 99, 100, 101, 102, 103, 104, 105, 107, 108, 109, 110, 111, 113, 114, 115, 116, 118, 119, 122, 123, 125, 126, 127, 128, 129, 131, 133, 134, 135, 136, 137, 138, 139, 141, 142, 143, 144, 145, 147, 148, 149, 150, 151, 152, 153, 154, 155, 156, 157, 159, 160, 161, 162, 163, 164, 165, 166, 169, 171, 173, 174, 175, 177, 178, 179, 180, 181, 182, 183, 184 center and bottom right, 185, 186, 187, 189

KELLY B. WILSON: 97